Communication

The Comprehensive Guide To Enhancing Your Influence, Communication Skills, And Personal Development

(Effective Communication And Conflict Resolution A Step-By-Step Guide)

Arno-Eric Krause

TABLE OF CONTENT

Chapter 1: The Fundamentals Of Conflict Resolution..........1

Chapter 2: How To Become A Compassionate Listener And Conversationalist..........10

Chapter 3: Improving Your Public Speaking Capabilities Developing A Robust And Distinct Speaking Voice..........18

Chapter 4: Do Not Shame Your Children In Public..........29

Chapter 5: Obstacles To Communication..........32

Chapter 6: How To Develop Confidence..........41

CHAPTER 7: Have Integrity..........51

Chapter 8: What Do We Specifically Mean By Power?..........59

Chapter 9: Setting Boundaries And Establishing Rules..........63

Chapter 10: Instructional Requirements..........68

Chapter 11: Create An Excellent First Impression..........77

Chapter 12: Creating An Outstanding Initial Impression When Meeting Your In-Laws..........90

Chapter 13: Fundamentals Of Interaction..........96

Chapter 14: Self-Assurance Does Not Come Naturally 116

Chapter 15: Avoid Making Assumptions 123

Chapter 1: The Fundamentals Of Conflict Resolution

The Cruciality of Reconciliation

Reconciliation is a more time-consuming and intricate interaction than seeking resolution. Reconciliation must take place during the resolution discussions; otherwise, it may never occur because the relationship will be irreparably damaged.

Reconciliation plays a role in the transformation of relationships, including those between team members and management. It entails numerous discussions long after the conflict has ended. These discussions can include documenting the events that led to the tension, reestablishing trust, and supporting all parties involved. This is important as it can strengthen relationships to a mutual acceptance of ideas, creating a stronger work bond.

Having an agreement in place during the post-conflict period will contribute to the security, comfort, and stability of future relationships. The success of reconciliation is contingent on ongoing communication throughout the conflict resolution process.

God's Heart on Resolving Conflict

Even the Bible acknowledges that people will not always live in harmony and anticipates conflict. There are numerous instances of conflict depicted in both Testaments. We can discuss the disputes between Cain and Abel, David and Goliath, Joseph and his brothers, Mary and Martha, and even the disciples. In light of this foresight, we are instructed on how to resolve our conflicts.

The expectation is that we will approach conflict with humility and forgiveness, while initiating a conversation with the person who is determined to be disagreeable. We are also expected to engage in self-reflection prior to resolution discussions.

Being Humble

The constant instruction of the Bible is to maintain humility. Due to our upbringing, humility is rarely viewed as a positive quality and may even be considered a flaw. We are frequently stubborn, unwilling to listen to the ideas of others, unable to empathise with the difficulties of others, and quick to anger. As a result of our reluctance to admit that we may be wrong in a given circumstance, these characteristics are significant obstacles to resolving conflict.

As a result of our humility, we will be able to take a step back and listen to the other person, not just to their words but also to the deeper aspects of their perspective.

Self-Reflection

To be humble, we must examine our own thoughts, emotions, and motivations. Luke 6:42 instructs us to first examine the beam in our own eyes before pointing out the speck in our brother's. This serves as a reminder that we should examine our own behaviours and motivations before criticising another person's actions. We must ask ourselves whether we are willing to forgive the other person, because only if we can affirm that we are can we expect the other person to forgive.

Our willingness to extend forgiveness will pave the way for reconciliation.

Apologies play a role

For our own healing, we must make a conscious decision to forgive. It is difficult to overcome feelings of anger, betrayal, and disappointment and decide to forgive.

The misconception regarding forgiveness and reconciliation is that you must be friends with the offender. Realizing that this person cannot or will not acknowledge their role in the conflict and, as a result, will not ask for your forgiveness is a daunting task. Forgiveness is the only action that can be performed from a distance, as it has no effect on the offender other than to relieve you of tension, anxiety, anger, bitterness, and other physical and mental health issues.

Forgiveness and reconciliation are ways for you to acknowledge that you've been harmed and that you've been able to move on from those emotions. It indicates that you've reconciled your feelings toward the other person to the point where you can decide if you'll allow them into your personal space, either emotionally or physically, or if you'd feel safer with no further contact. When you can think of the incident or the individual with nothing but compassion, you are ready to forgive or have successfully forgiven the incident.

Guidelines for Handling Conflict

Matthew 18:15-21 describes the method we must employ to manage conflict, and the instruction is explicit:

We must find a quiet place and speak with the individual in private. It would require integrity, persistence, and compassion.

If this fails, we must then bring in a mediator, such as a supervisor or manager, to provide an impartial ear to the dilemma.

The situation would then be escalated to the management committee or church elders, depending on the circumstances, for further mediation.

If the situation does not improve, you must end the relationship in order to protect your well-being from the relationship's toxicity.

It is essential that we do not involve third parties unless we cannot find a way to work together, and this is for the sole purpose of mediating between you and your partner in conflict. Regarding God, conflict resolution is not a choice but an expectation. It is a requirement of His command that we love one another as He has loved us: unconditionally and always forgiving.

Strategie de résolution des conflits

To resolve a tense situation amicably, you must implement certain long-term strategies that will benefit you and your team. These strategies should be durable enough to provide your team with direction for future events. This is essential when working with a team of diverse personalities and backgrounds.

These strategies are predicated primarily on how individuals choose to respond in a conflict situation.

Avoidance

A person will employ this tactic when they feel uneasy in conflict situations. They have a tendency to ignore or avoid the tension around them, and they may be resistant to engaging in conversation. This can result in a prolonged process and a deterioration of the conflict's conditions with no resolution.

Competition

When there is a conflict between two parties, it devolves into a competition in which each party strives to "win" by outperforming the other. This indicates that they will be overly confident and expect one party to win and the other to lose. The impossibility of negotiating a different viewpoint hinders the group's efforts to achieve the desired outcomes.

Accommodation

When you acquiesce to another person's expectations and refrain from expressing your own emotions and thoughts, you are engaging in the accommodation strategy. When you admit you were incorrect about something, it can help to defuse a tense situation. However, accommodating someone for the sake of maintaining peace can be detrimental. This may result in the inability to reach a resolution and alter the group's dynamic such that the less accommodating members drive the decision-making process.

Collaboration

When your team is cooperative and assertive collectively, the likelihood of a positive conflict resolution is high. This facilitates communication within the team, and each member feels as though their contribution is valued. This open discussion will generate an acceptable solution for all parties.

Compromise

Each team member compromises a portion of their preferences, allowing each member's suggestions to be considered and possibly implemented. This procedure gives the group a sense of fairness, even if nobody is entirely satisfied.

In an ideal world, everyone would be satisfied with the resolution of a conflict, but in reality, someone will be dissatisfied. The subsequent step is to ensure that a solution is found that everyone will accept, thereby achieving team cohesion and achieving the team's objectives.

Chapter 2: How To Become A Compassionate Listener And Conversationalist

Don't make judgements

The skill of listening is a valuable asset. Understanding someone's perspective and gaining insight into their message can be beneficial. When people are intent on passing judgement, they frequently miss the point the speaker is attempting to make. The art of listening requires genuine interest in what others have to say, regardless of whether you agree with them or would prefer they say something else. We form opinions because we believe we can perform better than others. The skill of listening enables you to be receptive to an alternative viewpoint, which you may find surprising or even enlightening.

Give individuals feedback

The art of effective communication is simply the ability to hear not only what a person says but also what they say. Do not be afraid to express your thoughts on what the other person has said. If it is positive, give them a compliment. If it is negative, inform them. If a person informs you that they cannot receive information from another individual in a particular format, let them know; this will allow you to find solutions to this problem and possibly prevent it from occurring.

Communication is an extremely potent tool. It can provide us with extraordinary opportunities and adventures. Communication is bidirectional; whatever you put into the universe, whether positive or negative, will always return to you. The same applies to communication; if you want others to trust you and feel comfortable sharing their problems and life experiences with you, you must reciprocate when they open up to you. If we send out specific signals or clues that we are unwilling to heed, people will shut down communication with us. This means they will stop sharing their thoughts and emotions with us because they do not trust us to listen without judging or interfering. Being a good listener is not always simple, but it can be one of the most rewarding skills you ever acquire. Listening more will make all the difference in your relationships, so don't squander the opportunity.

Being an empathetic listener involves focusing on the other person's intent and message. It involves being respectful in your speech, tone, and facial expressions. It also involves focusing on the individual's needs, wants, desires, and objectives. A good listener is receptive to what others have to say, asks pertinent questions when necessary, and expresses interest in hearing what they have to say. They will feel valued and accepted by the other individual. Being an empathetic listener requires more than just words; it also requires demonstrating personal and professional concern for others.

Being a good listener requires time and effort. It is not something that can be completed easily overnight. The art of listening entails not only hearing another person's words, but also understanding their intention. Good listeners will take the time necessary to comprehend what the other person is saying. They ensure they fully comprehend the message, regardless of how challenging or unsettling it may initially appear. It does not matter how long it takes to fully comprehend what someone is saying; they will do whatever is necessary to grasp the message.

To be an empathetic listener, one must prioritise the other person. It makes no difference what the other person says or how they say it. It only matters that their needs and wants are satisfied. Their emotions are more important than yours; it doesn't matter what you want as long as you can help them achieve their goals. The art of listening requires a willingness to accept others for who they are, flaws and all, without judging who they ought to be or ought to have been.

A good listener is nonjudgmental and receptive to all communication from others. They avoid jumping to conclusions and strive to maintain composure when communicating. They do not evaluate the content or delivery of others' speech. They accept the feelings and thoughts of others without becoming defensive or offended. A good listener is curious about what another person has to say, who they are, and their hopes, dreams, aspirations, and objectives.

Patience and an appreciation of human nature are essential components of the art of listening. It takes time to develop good listening skills. The art of listening requires undivided attention to the person with whom one is conversing. It involves understanding how their mind functions, absorbing what they have just said, and recognising all the emotions that may be guiding their actions and expressions. It also involves the ability to hear unspoken messages in addition to spoken ones.

Communication requires at least two individuals. However, this does not automatically make you a good listener. You will need someone who is willing to communicate their desires and allow you to comprehend their thoughts and emotions. A person who can give you feedback on your interpersonal communication skills so that you can learn what they think and feel. It would be ideal if you had someone who has faith in your abilities so that they can freely express themselves without fear of being misunderstood or misconstrued. A good listener ensures that the other person comprehends their message, regardless of how difficult or painful it may be. They express their sincerity and genuine concern so that the other person knows they care and their time is not wasted when conversing with them. This also demonstrates their desire to comprehend their individuality. A good listener is receptive to what the other person has to say and how they say it, and is willing to ask for clarification when necessary.

Being A Good Listener Involves Actively Listening And Determining What The Other Person Desires And Requires From You. It Involves Understanding

Their Goals And Allowing Them To Express Themselves And Their Emotions. It Also Requires Awareness Of The Other Person's Emotions. They May Be Reacting For Reasons Other Than Fear Or Anger. They Are Uncertain About Their Current Actions, Thoughts, And Emotions. No Matter What Is Causing Their Partner Discomfort Or Pain In Life, A Good Listener Will Discover This In Order To Better Comprehend And Support Them.

Chapter 3: Improving Your Public Speaking Capabilities Developing A Robust And Distinct Speaking Voice

Developing a strong, clear speaking voice is a crucial aspect of public speaking effectiveness. A strong speaking voice can help engage the audience and convey confidence, whereas a weak or unclear voice can make it difficult for the audience to understand the speech and keep their interest throughout.

Here are some suggestions for developing a powerful and distinct speaking voice:

Use good posture: Maintain a tall and confident stance while speaking to amplify your voice and boost your confidence.

Speak at a moderate pace: Speaking too quickly can be difficult for the audience to comprehend, while speaking too slowly can be monotonous. Aim for a moderate pace that facilitates audience comprehension.

Use appropriate volume: Speak loudly enough for the entire audience to hear you, but not so loudly that you strain your voice or become unintelligible.

Change your tone: Changing your voice's pitch can help maintain audience interest and emphasise key points.

Use appropriate vocal techniques: Voice projection, using pauses for emphasis, and speaking with inflection can all help improve your speech delivery.

Practice: The more a person practises their speech, the more confident and comfortable they will become with their delivery.

Developing a strong, clear speaking voice is a crucial aspect of public speaking effectiveness. By using good posture, speaking at a moderate pace, using appropriate volume, varying pitch, and regularly practising, individuals can develop the skills and self-assurance necessary to speak with a strong, clear voice.

Effective use of body language and eye contact

Body language and eye contact are essential components of effective public speaking. Body language and eye contact can help engage the audience and communicate confidence, whereas poor body language and eye contact can detract from the speech's message.

Here are some tips for public speaking using effective body language and eye contact:

Use open body language to convey confidence and openness. Stand with your arms at your sides or use open hand gestures. Avoid crossing your arms or legs, as doing so can convey hostility or discomfort.

Utilize facial expressions to convey emotion and captivate the audience. Avoid using expressions that may seem unnatural or forced.

Maintain eye contact: Make eye contact with the audience to demonstrate engagement and establish rapport. Avoid looking down or away from the audience, as doing so can communicate a lack of confidence or interest.

Movement can help engage the audience and add variety to your speech delivery. Movement that is excessive or distracting can detract from the message of a speech.

The more a person practises their speech, the more at ease and assured they will be with their body language and eye contact.

Developing captivating and well-structured presentations

Presentations that are engaging and well-organized are an essential element of effective public speaking. A presentation that is well-organized can help maintain the audience's interest and make it easier for them to follow and comprehend the material.

Here are some suggestions for developing engaging and well-structured presentations:

Determine the presentation's purpose: Is the objective to inform, persuade, or entertain? Understanding the presentation's purpose will aid in determining its content and structure.

Collect and organise the information: Create an outline to organise the gathered information in a logical and understandable manner.

Think about the audience: Who will participate in the presentation? What are their histories, interests, and requirements? Adapt the presentation's content and structure to the audience.

Utilize visual aids: Visual aids, such as slides, graphs, and images, can help engage the audience and improve the presentation's delivery.

Use appropriate structure: To organise the presentation, use a clear introduction, body, and conclusion. Consider using transitions to connect ideas and maintain the presentation's flow.

Practice: The more a person practises their presentation, the more at ease and assured they will be when delivering it.

Handling difficult questions and situations

Effective public speaking requires the ability to respond to challenging questions and situations. Unanticipated, controversial, or confrontational questions or situations can be categorised as challenging.

Here are some suggestions for addressing challenging questions and situations when speaking publicly:

It is essential to maintain composure when confronted with a challenging question or situation. Take a deep breath and strive to maintain a neutral or upbeat attitude.

Recognize the question: Restating or summarising the question demonstrates your attentiveness and comprehension.

Answer truthfully: Be straightforward and honest in your response, but avoid becoming aggressive or defensive.

If the question or situation is sensitive or controversial, you should respond with tact and diplomacy. Avoid being combative and dismissive.

Humor is an effective tool for diffusing tension and diffusing difficult situations. Utilize it judiciously and sparingly.

Take a break: If the question or situation is especially challenging, it may be beneficial to take a break to collect your thoughts or consult with colleagues before responding.

Effective public speaking requires the ability to respond to challenging questions and situations. Individuals can effectively and confidently navigate difficult questions and situations by remaining calm, acknowledging the question, responding truthfully, using tact, and, when appropriate, employing humour.

Successful Correspondence via Telephone

Telephone conversations can be a quick way to get things done, but they can also leave room for confusion if you're not clear about what you want to discuss at the outset and what you hope to achieve as a result of the conversation.

It is a wonderful place to visit, but occasionally you may find yourself going in circles. You may also appear to agree to a particular action step, only to discover that the person you were speaking with has forgotten that portion of the conversation. This means that you could anticipate something crucial to occur, but it will never occur.

The best way to handle telephone conversations is to schedule as much time in advance as possible. Determine their level of interest and request a follow-up call at a convenient time, or an email address where you can reach them, if you need to make "cold pitches" - that is, calls to individuals you don't know in order to attempt to collaborate with them.

Don't attempt to advance like a charging bull. You may receive a negative response, leaving you with no opportunity for a substantive discussion. People are active, particularly columnists. If you are attempting to pitch a story to them, for example, and you call them when they are on cutoff time and immediately launch into your pitch, you will likely receive a "no, and don't call again."

However, if you call and inquire whether it is a good time to speak and whether they are on a deadline, they will recognise that you comprehend their working conditions and time constraints. If you believe you may want to pitch a story, ask when it would be a good time to contact them and whether they would prefer to be contacted by phone or email.

If you intend to make a subsequent call, you should be organised. Before every call, jot down ideas. Confirm each one separately. Depending on the situation, make notes.

Utilize transcription software, such as dictation.io, if you are concerned that you may overlook something. While the facts indicate that you may have the option to record your side of the conversation, in this manner you will have your side of the story. Depending on the situation, you can take notes about what they say.

After the discussion has concluded, review your notes and type them so that they appear acceptable. Once you are certain you have an accurate summary of what was reviewed, send a thank-you email to the individual. Send a copy of the notes you have created.

Specify any activity steps, deadlines, or subsequent gatherings that must be observed. In this manner, you can ensure that you are in complete agreement with the disclosed information. You can also inquire if you missed anything or if there was anything else they needed to review. Request that they include it in the email or organise a second call.

After they have provided their feedback, you will receive a standardised report and "documentation" containing the primary topics that were discussed during the call. Then, you can use it to track progress, make new agreements, modify existing ones, etc.

This is a refreshing shift toward the significance of written communication as a component of your overall initiative strategies. How about we examine this in the segment that follows?

Chapter 4: Do Not Shame Your Children In Public.

Have you ever severely reprimanded your child in a public place for something he did or how he behaved? Has this manner of yours evolved into a habit? If so, you should immediately cease doing so. Freely disgracing your children can do more damage to their reputation than you can imagine. The following are five reasons why you should never do such a thing:

Could encourage harassing conduct Your child's dominant, obnoxious behaviour may be prompted by public disgrace. A child's psyche is like a speck of dirt, and he absorbs everything he sees. Assuming you frequently correct or reprimand him in broad daylight, he could do the same among his peers. This will essentially serve as a method for him to vent his frustration, which should be avoided at all costs.

2. Immense shame

Your child may experience extreme humiliation if he or she is rebuked in broad daylight in the presence of witnesses. Nobody wants to look terrible in public, and the same goes for your child. Even if your child has committed a grave error, you should avoid attacking him openly.

3. Lost trust

Regarding the relationship between a parent and a child, it is essential to build and maintain a foundation of trust. If your child frequently observes you reprimanding him in broad daylight, even for minor offences, he may lose trust in you. He will conceal information, become defiant, and may attempt to begin communicating with you.

4. impact on fundamental well-being

You should instruct your child not to repeat a similar error. You should either engage in cordial conversation with him or privately reprimand him. Public disgrace will only exacerbate your child's misery, disappointment, and distress. To maintain your child's self-assurance, it is recommended that you speak to him in private.

5. Regret later

You may have been overcome with outrage at the time you assaulted your child, but you will have second thoughts later. Typically, children conduct themselves in public in ways that can irritate adults. Ensure you remind yourself not to express your annoyance without much consideration. You can reprimand your child about the incident when you return home, but openly criticizing him will only exacerbate the situation.

Chapter 5: Obstacles To Communication

How do disputes arise? They frequently occur when we allow our emotions to cloud our judgement or when we misunderstand someone. By having a "negative listening attitude," we erect barriers that impede communication. These obstacles must be acknowledged, eliminated, or overcome for communication to once again flow freely.

Among the communication barriers we face are the following:

Others who are attempting to interact with you, such as clients or coworkers, will feel neglected and irritated if you allow yourself to become distracted. By demonstrating disrespect and unprofessionalism by ignoring them, communication will be severed. This could result in losing a client, having a boss complain about you, or losing respect. Maintain your focus on what is being said and give your client or coworker your complete attention. Do not permit yourself to become distracted. If you must leave the chat to take a call or speak with a colleague, please apologise.

- Not making eye contact: It is essential to make eye contact with the person with whom you are conversing. It displays your inquisitiveness and attention to detail. By not looking at the other person while they are speaking, you are demonstrating a lack of attention and making them feel uncomfortable. They may conclude that you are dishonest or unreliable and are concealing information from them.

Interrupting a speaker is a significant barrier to effective two-way communication and may lead to conflict. You are once again expressing your disinterest in what they have to say. It is impossible to fully comprehend the desires and expectations of another person if you interrupt them to express your own ideas or, even worse, if you finish their sentences. Allow them to finish their sentence before responding. Take charge of the discussion by posing leading or closing questions that accept only succinct responses if it must be cut short for any reason.

Assuming you are aware of another person's desires can also be problematic. For instance, the fact that a customer enters your business wearing a t-shirt and torn pants does not indicate that they will be unable to pay for your goods or services. Permit your clients and colleagues to express their needs without prompting or directing.

Voice tone: During a conversation, the tone of one's voice has the potential to spark conflict. People may react negatively to a voice with an arrogant, demanding, angry, or whining tone. Maintain a respectful, tranquil, and pleasant tone when speaking with clients or coworkers. At the very least, try to maintain a neutral tone of voice if you are irritated.

- Sarcasm: Sarcasm invites conflict and has no place in a discussion between two people. Everyone has moments at work when they feel as though they'll lose their minds if they receive any more ridiculous questions or comments, but responding with sarcasm only makes the other person feel worse and may even lower their self-esteem. We frequently forget that not everyone is as knowledgeable about our industry as we are; in fact, the majority of consumers have only a passing familiarity with the industries in which they work.

Therefore, we may excuse our clients or less-experienced employees for posing questions with straightforward answers that are only apparent to those in the know. Being patient and understanding is much simpler and more enjoyable than responding in a sarcastic or insulting manner.

- Rudeness: There is never a valid reason to be rude. You should avoid or diffuse any hostility a client may bring into your office by maintaining a professional and courteous demeanour. However, if you are working with a client with whom you simply cannot get along, being unpleasant is not the solution. In a conversation, request guidance from your boss or supervisor.

- Cultural differences: cultural differences can lead to a variety of disputes. It is simple to misinterpret words, gestures, and traditions when conversing with people of various nationalities and religious beliefs. If you wish to achieve success in your field, you should familiarise yourself with some of the most prevalent cultural practises. In general, however, polite and respectful behaviour is well received by people of various backgrounds and beliefs. Never make fun of cultural practises with which you are unfamiliar. Respect everyone with whom you interact, including your clients and coworkers.

Which of the two attitudes toward listening, positive or negative, will produce the desired results?

Effectively Utilizing Communication

Now that you understand the fundamentals of communication, it is time to consider how to utilise it effectively by selecting the appropriate channel for your intended audience. Before choosing the appropriate approach and level of formality, you decide with whom you wish to speak.

Acceptable Tone and Expression

The manner in which you interact with coworkers and clients will depend on a variety of factors, including the tone of your voice, the sophistication of your language, and the form of address you use. It is essential to take into account how well you know the individual.

Your communication style will vary significantly based on how well you know the person you are speaking with. When conversing with someone you know well, such as a colleague or a regular client, you may use their first name, use less professional language and tone, make jokes, etc.

When interacting with an unfamiliar person, you must adopt a more formal and professional demeanour. While it may be acceptable to call someone by their first name and make jokes with a younger person, it is inappropriate to do so with an elderly person. Unless they specifically request otherwise, use their title and last name when addressing them, such as "Good morning, Mr. Smith." Your relationship with them Again, it is acceptable to be friendly when interacting with known individuals, but professionalism is required when interacting with clients, senior staff members, and others who may affect the image of your organisation. These individuals require a professional and courteous demeanour when interacting with you.

An investigation into culture. In today's world, it is not uncommon to interact with people from all walks of life and all corners of the globe; therefore, it is important to consider their level of English when conversing, especially with people from different cultures. Avoid using lengthy and difficult terms. Use straightforward and concise language whenever possible.

If you frequently interact with people from different countries, such as in a hotel or airport, you should become familiar with ways to address them and other practises that will help them feel more at ease. For instance, it is polite to offer a brief bow when speaking to a Japanese person, but it is impolite to make prolonged eye contact with a Middle Eastern person.

Chapter 6: How To Develop Confidence

Confidence is not innate; rather, it is something that is acquired through experience. If you observe someone with a great deal of self-confidence, they have worked diligently over time to cultivate it. Self-assurance is earned, not given

Negative comments, business failures, and redundancies are a few examples of circumstances that can lower a victim's self-esteem. Even when they have good intentions, people can make you feel insecure by making offensive remarks.

In addition, there is self-doubt, which is the belief that you are unworthy of success and therefore unable to complete a task. The following actions are required for one to develop self-confidence:

Make an employee list.

Creating a list of one's abilities necessitates noting the skills one believes to possess. When using this method, one must include every detail and leave nothing out.

Do you tell tales effectively? Do you strive for excellence? Do you sing while taking the shower? These items must appear on the list. Always consider the mentioned concerns, and be proud of yourself. Do not be ashamed to boast about your achievements to your friends and coworkers.

Learn How to Acknowledge Compliments

Accepting compliments demonstrates maturity. The size of the contribution is more important than its source. if the compliment is genuine and not something you were forced to accept. When complimented, say "thank you" with sincerity.

Instead of rejecting the compliment, believe in your own value and take pride in it. The compliments increase your confidence. Instead of assuming the praise you receive from coworkers or friends is sarcastic, have self-confidence and accept it. Accepting it after years of self-doubt may be difficult at first, but with practise, one can gain mastery.

Education

Someone who takes pride in their knowledge or who reads many books will be confident. Increase your confidence by being aware of your surroundings, underlying issues, and familiar reading materials. Although it is not necessary to be an expert in the subject, having some knowledge of it can be beneficial. Discover the subjects that your coworkers and friends find fascinating. This can be achieved through the study of fashion, politics, business, and sports. Newspapers, periodicals, sports broadcasts, current topics, and newspapers all contain information.

Try a little risk and be receptive to novel concepts.

Embracing new ideas and embarking on new adventures can also contribute to one's sense of self-assurance. What matters is how you implement your ideas in practise. putting oneself to the test by travelling to different countries and engaging in activities such as eating Chinese food, camping, watching NASCAR, and climbing mountains. At least twice per month, it is recommended to experiment with new ideas. Even if you don't enjoy one experience, don't immediately give up; instead, try another one. Over time, self-assurance grows.

Exercising and Eating Well

One can maintain their body in a variety of ways outside of the gym. Morning jogs and swimming are two exercises that can be performed at home or in the neighbourhood. Another option is to seek assistance from a gym trainer. A healthy diet can also improve mental and physical health. Consuming junk food can be detrimental to your health and even reduce your self-esteem. The regimen should consist of consuming large quantities of water and switching from unhealthy (junk food) to healthy foods (fruits and vegetables). A healthy diet and regular exercise can increase a person's self-confidence and pride in their accomplishments.

Alter the Individuals You Surround Yourself With There are certain people who make you feel consistently unworthy, voiceless, and full of negativity. Even if they are close friends or family members, you must severe ties with these individuals. Replace them with someone who inspires hope and recognises your potential. Someone who makes you feel secure and safe while in their presence. You owe it to yourself to try, even if making new acquaintances and parting with a longtime friend can be difficult. These new people have the potential to provide you with the encouragement you need to gain confidence gradually.

Dancing for Personal Entertainment

When dancing, the brain releases a hormone that aids in stress management. You can dance in public or at home to your favourite music. It does not matter where you are as long as you have fun dancing. Instead of considering what others are saying, consider yourself. You will be adored for who you are; you may even surprise yourself.

Complete Closet Remodeling

Try on some outfits that are stylistically distinct from your typical wardrobe. A change of clothes can be advantageous. Try on some new clothing, jeans, suits, shirts, deodorant, fragrances, and other accessories. Allow your loved ones to assist you in selecting outfits that flatter your figure when you go shopping with them. Changing your entire wardrobe is still possible on a tight budget and without going overboard. When a person looks good, their self-assurance increases.

Try to accomplish more difficult tasks.

This strategy may seem odd to a great number of people, but over time it increases one's confidence. By accepting additional responsibilities and undertaking additional work, one tests his or her capacity. As a result of completing these assignments, you will meet members of the organisation.

Recognize and appreciate Others

This strategy involves being helpful to those around you. As you work on your confidence, you realise that another person is experiencing the same problem. Be their guide and encourage them to build their self-assurance. Take the time to say thank you to your coworkers and family members who assisted you during your transition.

Adopt a positive attitude and never surrender

Don't give up when attempting to do something. Even if the exercise becomes difficult, make every effort to continue. Your desired outcome may be around the corner. Every problem has a solution; you simply need to know where to look. When a person accomplishes something, they experience a sensation that increases their confidence.

Constantly negative thinking and being told that one cannot succeed can erode confidence. Continue to think positively about your situation and the steps you intend to take to rectify it. Don't give up, even if the objective you've set for yourself becomes more challenging along the way. Have confidence in your own value and ability. You become what you believe, so if you tell yourself that you are not attractive, not good enough, or weak and unable to succeed, you will become those things. However, if you consistently have positive thoughts about yourself, your confidence will grow.

Having knowledge.

Learn more about the tasks you set out to accomplish, whether at home or at the office. Due to their confidence, someone who is well-prepared for an exam is more likely to succeed than someone who is unprepared.

CHAPTER 7: Have Integrity

After a negotiation, it is frequently difficult to determine the quality of the deal you have obtained. If we evaluated our performance without factoring in self-justification, this would be much easier to determine. Have you ever wondered, "If I had performed differently or made different decisions, would I have gotten a better deal?" It is simple to move on without evaluating our performance, the what and why, and the overall quality of the agreement. Learning something from each negotiation guarantees that you will benefit from the encounter, even if unanticipated concessions occur. This requires being honest with yourself. The following four categories provide a useful framework for evaluating and preparing for your next negotiation.

The four challenges we confront

The initial obstacle is all about you.

Negotiation is uncomfortable. It often requires silence, threats, and punishments, which many individuals find difficult to execute effectively. To perform effectively, you must accept responsibility for your actions and recognise the substantial impact your performance can have on every agreement in which you are engaged.

Negotiation is a skill that can be learned and used, but you must be self-motivated and flexible. It is not enough to be tough or prepared. It is most important to be motivated by the promise of producing value and profit through well-considered agreements. As a result, you should recognise that past success is no guarantee of future success, especially because every negotiation, like every basketball or football game, is unique.

Therefore, the first task falls to you. People negotiate, not robots or corporations. We all have biases, perspectives, beliefs, preferences, pressures, goals, and opinions, and so will the other side in your negotiations. As part of our journey, you will discover why your greatest obstacle in negotiation is yourself and how, by nature, you see the world through your own eyes rather than through the eyes of others.

To discover how others perceive the world and what their goals are when marketing and negotiating, it is essential to conduct exploratory meetings, exercise patience, and seek to work with the other party rather than assuming and imposing one's own views. To be an effective negotiator, you must be able to comprehend the dynamics of any scenario from "within" the opposing party's mind. Without this knowledge, you will remain in a state known as "being inside your own head," which is a terrible negotiating position. If you truly want to negotiate effectively, you must first alter your mindset.

Due to the proliferation of smartphones and other electronic devices, vehicle wiring may soon become obsolete. This Bluetooth device can operate the vehicle's lights, fuel flap, windows, and ignition. Although the electrical equipment was not unique, the software was, and ETD had begun training and marketing its benefits. Thomas Schnider, director of sales for ETD, met with the procurement staff at Brionary, a major supplier of auto components. He presented a meticulously organised business case that justified the higher price point by demonstrating how their product could save money in other areas.

ETD acknowledged that such a modification would not be considered until the next generation of vehicles. Their excitement about this opportunity prevented them from entering the minds of Brionary's clients. Brionary posed the questions listed below.

Can we purchase our own access to the software and programme?

We purchase the majority of our electronics from vendors in which we have a financial interest.

"How do we overcome this difficulty?"

3. "How long do you anticipate it will take to copy this type of software?"

Most likely, the solution will be implemented before the next generation of automobiles hits the market.

Thomas and his team returned to their headquarters in Cologne to reconsider their strategy. They had considered the possibility of negotiating terms in their own minds. After one month, they granted Brionary access to the software in exchange for a contract extension on their current hardware components. If they had been in Brionary's mind, who was obviously receptive to long-term co-investment, they might have taken a different approach.

No rules govern negotiations. There are no established protocols, and there are no cans or cannots. Sometimes, negotiation is compared to a game of chess, with the exception that in most talks, you are not necessarily attempting to defeat your opponent and are not restricted to a limited number of possible moves. Although there are no absolute rules for negotiation, we can work within certain constraints. The majority of negotiators are granted bargaining authority by their supervisor, but only up to a certain point, after which conversations typically escalate. Total autonomy exposes individuals to danger and risk, which is typically inappropriate.

Recognizing your accomplishments.

How will you know how well you bargained? You won't, because the other party is unlikely to tell you how you could have performed better or how well you did relative to their other options.

Therefore, in the absence of input from those with whom we negotiate, we must rely on historical precedents (the outcome of the previous round) or absolute measures (our profit-and-loss statement) and be humble enough to ask, What should I have done differently? Could I have made different decisions? Could I have said something different?

Could I have submitted better-considered proposals?

Could I have agreed with greater ease in the end?

This type of question tests your honesty with yourself. All of the conditions must be considered when defining a fair agreement. When the legitimacy of a transaction is questioned, our ego may cause us to assign blame to external factors. Upon completion of a transaction, you may wish to move on to implementation rather than reflect on your performance.

Chapter 8: What Do We Specifically Mean By Power?

You are only as powerful as others perceive you to be, which can be discouraging if you do not comprehend how others perceive the issue. Power can be real or perceived, and it can be subjective or objective in the sense that it exists in people's minds regardless of whether the other person is dependent on you or not. Power can shift, develop with time and environment, and be used to nurture or abuse. It is obvious that comprehension and appreciation are required.

Why is a power balance so crucial?

So, what role does power play in negotiations? Simply put, it provides options and, once understood, enables you to choose where on the clock face your discussion will occur.

- Maintaining power balance. If you hold the balance of power in your relationship(s), you have greater control over the agenda, the negotiation process, and the negotiation itself. Impact on the environment, style, strategy, and possibilities. Depending on your goals and objectives, power allows you to choose whether to be competitive or cooperative.

It is possible to create the illusion of power prior to the start of a negotiation by displaying disinterest, describing your alternatives, or highlighting the opponent's lack of options. All of these are designed to manage expectations and give the impression that you are negotiating from a position of strength. Attempting to do so after conversations have begun is unnecessary and may be futile. The Completely Skilled Negotiator is aware of the need to precisely communicate the situation's facts to the parties involved in order to increase their perceived authority.

Maintaining a power balance

Historiography demonstrates that those with power will at some point attempt to utilise it. Consequently, it is essential to comprehend the power dynamic, identify the anticipated location of the discussion on the clock face, and plan accordingly. How and where you negotiate on the clock face will be directly affected by the type of relationship you have with the individuals you negotiate with.

When assessing power, the amount of information available about each party's situation will be one of the most important factors to consider. The degree to which time and circumstances are transparent has a direct bearing on the power dynamic in your relationship and the type of negotiation that will likely ensue. That is not to say, however, that those in a weak position enter negotiations as lambs ready to be slaughtered: frequently, the more powerful party will use the situation to gain other forms of value, such as loyalty, exclusivity, or greater flexibility, as opposed to simply beating the other party into agreeing to a lower price. The location of your negotiations on the clock face will affect all of these options and the overall value potential of your negotiations. Therefore, if we are to maximise power, we must treat it with reverence. The objective is not to win or defeat the opposition. They are not your competition. Its purpose is to help you maximise the effectiveness of the discussions you are preparing for.

Chapter 9: Setting Boundaries And Establishing Rules

Parenting involves numerous facets, such as establishing norms and limits. They give children a sense of stability and order and assist them in understanding what is expected of them. Boundaries and rules also aid parents in establishing limits and directing their children's behaviour, which may foster happier and more harmonious family relationships.

When rearing a child, there are a variety of methods for establishing limits and guidelines. One strategy is to be specific and consistent with your expectations. This entails stating explicitly what actions are permitted and prohibited and enforcing the norms consistently. It is essential, for instance, to consistently enforce your rules regarding your child's arrival home from school on school evenings and to avoid making exceptions. This shows your child that you take your words seriously and expect them to adhere to the rules.

Being just and stern also aids in establishing limits and regulations. This involves establishing and consistently upholding boundaries that are fair and appropriate for your child's age and stage of development. Even if your child begs or asks you to make an exception, you must consistently enforce your rules and not give in to exception-seeking conduct. This will teach your child that you are in charge and they must follow your rules.

It is also essential to be consistent with your punishments when enforcing rules and regulations. This involves enforcing the punishments you previously established for specific conduct. It is essential to consistently enforce the consequence of not allowing your child to watch television if, for example, they must complete their homework before watching television. This helps to emphasise the importance of following the rules and teaches your child that there are consequences for breaking them.

Setting limits and adopting guidelines regarding screen time may be beneficial. Many parents find it challenging to limit the amount of time their child spends in front of a screen, whether for television, computer use, or video games. To ensure that your child does not spend too much time in front of a screen and to encourage them to engage in other activities such as reading, playing outside, and spending time with family and friends, it is necessary to impose restrictions on screen time. To create boundaries and rules surrounding screen time, you can limit the amount of time your child can spend using screens each day, designate times when screens are prohibited, or impose restrictions on the types of content they are permitted to watch or play.

Creating boundaries and establishing norms regarding domestic duties and responsibilities could be advantageous in a different circumstance. Many parents struggle to get their children to pitch in around the house and accept responsibility for their actions. You could assign specific tasks to each child, establish due dates for tasks, and establish consequences for not completing tasks in order to establish boundaries and regulations regarding household duties. If your child repeatedly fails to clean his or her room, you might forbid him or her from watching television until the room is organised. This teaches your child responsibility for their actions and that breaking the law has consequences.

In conclusion, establishing limits and standards are essential aspects of parenting that can contribute to a sense of stability, peace, and order within the family. By being clear and consistent with your expectations, firm and fair with your limitations, and consistent with your punishments, you can successfully set limits and standards that will help guide your child's behaviour and foster a pleasant and respectful relationship between you and your child.

Chapter 10: Instructional Requirements

You should avoid using phrases such as "paradise on earth" that sound appealing but do not actually help people enjoy themselves. Because sentences with excessively irregular language make it difficult to comprehend your message. Then, to ensure their comprehension, you must describe in great detail. Or, people may repeatedly furrow their brows when speaking.

Use caution when employing a new or contemporary expression. Do not make the other person feel uneasy or uncomfortable. These are advantages that cannot be attained by speaking in a normal, everyday manner.

Unimportant Words

Words that are not part of our vocabulary but that confuse what we are attempting to communicate and cause others to hear unimportant information can be quite harmful at times. A listening session. Then why do we speak these words? They resemble crutches, which are required to prevent limping.

Numerous English speakers have a propensity for repeatedly saying "you know." How about that? is how one of my Washington, DC-based friends always begins a statement. A different acquaintance, aware of this practise, made an effort to count the number of times he used the phrase in a 20-minute meeting. According to statistics, "You know what" appears 91 times! That means the man in Washington will say "you know" approximately four and a half times per minute. I am uncertain as to whether the 91-word phrase "you know" or the discussion's topics are more enduring. If you take the story model seriously, despite its absurdity, the problem is concerning. Could the "you know" guy communicate effectively if he allowed the habit to take over? A minor habit that could cause minor harm. Not to mention how extremely bored the audience is. However, do you frequently begin your sentences with "you know"?

Use caution when beginning sentences with "essentially," "typically," "anyway," and "hopefully" (hopefully). ... Try paying close attention the next time you are watching the evening news to see if the announcer repeats these phrases. Notify "Guinness World Records" if you observe that each sentence contains only one word.

In fact, I concur that it is sometimes necessary to emphasise a point using these expressions. Although your intention is to simply announce that the party will be held tomorrow night, it is not a good idea to go overboard with phrases such as "I hope to host a party tomorrow night." Consequently, is the word "hopefully" necessary? Moreover, individuals will interpret your message differently.

Try to avoid overusing words in your sentences, regardless of the subject matter. These words can be harmful when they "sneak" into a discourse. Close your mouth and say exactly what you mean.

USE EXACT LANGUAGE

Given the wide variety of modern uses of the word, this issue is not easily resolved. I am ashamed to bring up this topic. However, we also make an effort to research and evaluate it, whether we like it or not.

The precise selection of words can reveal something about the status of the speaker or their attitude toward society in general. There are outmoded values and judgements in a rapidly changing society. As an illustration, I use the fact that women now play a larger role in society. So, is it acceptable to call them "weak sex"? Back then, black people were frequently described with racial slurs. Numerous professions are currently dominated by people of colour, particularly in sports. Similarly, the importance of the right to equality without discrimination is growing. Historically referred to as "black slaves," the term "African American" is now required. Currently, the correct term is "Asian," whereas in the past it was "yellow-skinned orientals" (Asian). formerly known as "Hispanic," Latino is now the preferred term. Any ethnic community desires to be addressed with respect by their origin name. The Washington Post once published a list of the names of immigrants who entered the country over time in order to demonstrate progress. In 1987, the term "African-American" appeared 42 times in a single publication; by 1993, its occurrence had increased to 1,422 times.

This information demonstrates how far we have progressed in the intellectual war. Words have evolved to express greater respect for numerous peoples. Carelessness with the appropriate language will place you at a significant disadvantage.

Exists a distinction between scepticism and trust? Is there a reason for our reluctance to replace "female" with "lady"? Obviously, not every woman qualifies as a lady. Nevertheless, the word has been recognised. You have the choice of using or not using. This issue was presented by a female editor of a small magazine and another male editor.

You may be a bit hasty when you tell a female coworker in the workplace, "You look incredible in this blouse!" or "This outfit makes you so attractive!" It is currently advised to exercise caution when offering praise. The greatest compliment is "This dress is beautiful!"

However, does it not also appear moderate and "remaining"? However, it is safe. Safety is currently the most important factor. The film "The King and I" contains the phrase "What is there is there" (The King and I). No is not what is. Now, however, everything is in chaos. Throughout the film, the king's comments are humorous but not completely absurd. What transpired? Things that were once stigmatised are now accepted. Some things that were acceptable in the past are now unacceptable. In addition, the contemporary word sea is disorganised. Therefore, using inappropriate language can be detrimental.

Eliminate your awful speech-reading habits.

How do you implement poor behaviour? Remember these three strategies:

Simply put, pay attention to the first words that come out of your mouth. You must monitor your own speech while speaking. You must be aware of when to stop and when to proceed. How frequently have you paused before saying "Well, uh"? These are the worms that produce your speech.

Second, prepare what you will say prior to speaking. I am aware of how challenging this is. We occasionally forget to complete a phrase, which causes us anxiety. I do not imply that you must compose an entire speech before stepping up to the microphone. Nevertheless, you can formulate the second statement while delivering the first. If you find this task too difficult, try practising more. Then, you'll realise that it's entirely possible, and you'll soon have to master it. You can certainly conjure up two issues simultaneously. If we understand how to use our brain, it can be extraordinarily useful.

Third, create a "check board" to monitor your speech and quickly correct any errors. The "Inspection Board" will immediately communicate "Stop or Zap" - (Stop or Continue!) to you. Who is the "inspection board"? Are any of your friends seated in the section beneath you? By their glances and subtle hand movements, you can determine the nature of the situation. This has an unanticipated outcome. Friends' support means that you are not speaking alone and can do so with assurance. I guarantee that you will acquire a flawless command of the English language with consistent practise.

Chapter 11: Create An Excellent First Impression

According to experts, we make snap judgements about new people within thirty seconds to two minutes.

Elliott Abrams

First impressions are the initial judgements we form upon meeting a new person. These judgements are based on the individual's mannerisms, how they speak, how they dress, and a multitude of other factors that range from vague and superficial to profound and intuitive.

To gain a reasonable level of understanding of someone, you must spend a considerable amount of time with them. No reasonable person will judge a person solely on the basis of a first impression, but there are times when you must impress your audience quickly. First impressions draw conclusions without waiting or asking why. When we form a first impression of someone, our mind paints a detailed picture of what we should expect from them without our being aware of the underlying mechanisms.

As you read this chapter, keep in mind that creating a positive first impression is all about being yourself. First impressions are frequently influenced by a variety of superficial qualities. When we are at ease and feel like we belong, we naturally exude a positive first impression.

On the first meeting, no one expects to gain insights into your soul, so the objective is to demonstrate authenticity. This can manifest as courtesy, interest, and self-assurance. People are very good at picking out inauthentic behaviour and the only sure way to spoil your first impression is to present a false image of yourself. A first impression is not an opportunity to sell yourself; rather, it is an opportunity to allow people to warm up to you and vice versa.

Creating a Positive First Impression During an Interview

People form instantaneous judgements about you. In an interview, you must overcome your nerves and let your genuine personality shine through. A surprising number of corporate HR managers and small business owners admit to placing greater emphasis on cultural compatibility than on professional experience when hiring new talent. Most job postings receive hundreds, if not thousands, of applicants; therefore, being likeable during an interview is extremely important. If the interviewer believes that you will be easy to work with, you have an excellent chance of landing the position over a candidate who is more qualified. If they had a pleasant conversation with you and believe you are willing to do whatever it takes to develop the necessary skills for the position, they are more likely to advance you in the hiring process.

Find a way to relax, regardless of how tense you are, without appearing flippant. If your potential future boss is interviewing you, he or she is likely not an expert in interviewing; rather, they are an expert in their field. Assume that, unless you're being interviewed by Oprah, the person conducting the interview may lack confidence in their abilities in this field. Because there is no science behind this, they may only interview a few individuals per year and are likely to ask stock questions. The majority of interviewers are somewhat uneasy when conducting them. Be genuine and show your true colours while attempting to learn as much as possible about your interviewer.

Use the following advice to ace your next interview:

1. Pay attention to the Interviewer

Focus on the interviewer, as they are the most important individual at this time. You must give them your complete focus. Do not oversell yourself by speaking more than you listen. Be sincere in your desire to obtain the position.

You can ask the interviewer directly what they require most from the job description. Consider all of their requirements. To demonstrate that you have been paying attention, ask questions that are tailored to each informational need. Getting them to discuss their business will make them more at ease with you. This is an excellent opportunity to learn more about the position for which you are applying. Always keep an eye out for potential red flags, as these can lead to excellent follow-up questions.

Now that you are aware of their needs, you should describe the skills, experiences, and personality traits you possess that match their requirements. Be tactful when discussing areas where experience is lacking. You don't have to come right out and admit your deficiencies, but you should express confidence that you'll be able to acquire any skills you're not completely proficient with. All that matters is authenticity. Maintain a confident physique, make eye contact, and smile when appropriate. Maintain eye contact throughout the interview, whether in person or online. This demonstrates that you are confident and attentive to what they are saying.

2. Keep Your Composure

Maintain proper posture and show genuine interest in each interviewer. Avoid becoming disoriented, preoccupied, or camera shy. I enjoy the expression never let them see you sweat. Maintain focus.

You can take comfort in the fact that the interviewer cares as much as you do about selecting the best candidate for the job. If you have an in-person interview, sit up straight and avoid slouching, pull your shoulders back, and keep your cool throughout the process. If you notice that you are fidgeting, control it but don't overthink it. Obsessing over anything negative you observe about yourself can sabotage an otherwise successful interview, whereas displaying uncomfortable body language will not hurt your chances of landing the job. Remember that the only reason you were invited to the interview is because you are likely the best candidate for the position.

When participating in a video interview, ensure that the sound, lighting, and video quality are all excellent. To reflect your personality, the background should be neat and organised. Before logging in, activate the camera to ensure that you are not backlit and that nothing distracting is in the field of view. Ensure that everyone around you is aware of the situation to reduce the likelihood of distraction. If you are interrupted during the interview, this is an excellent opportunity to demonstrate how you respond when things do not go as planned. Keep your cool, maintain your concentration, and be cordial.

3. Ask Questions

You should enter the interview with a few questions prepared based on your research of the company and the position.

You can direct your first question at the interviewer to establish rapport. You could inquire as to why they chose to work for the organisation and what they enjoy most about its culture. Determine what they like about their job. Ask if they have any advice for someone in your position who is just starting out at the company.

4. Reflect the behaviour of the interviewer

Matching your communication style to that of your interviewer can help move things along. Some people speak quickly and abruptly, whereas others speak slowly. Observe the interviewer's cadence and mirror it back to them.

If your interviewer speaks slowly and clearly, you should also speak slowly and clearly. This will give them the impression that they have found someone similar to themselves, which will make them feel more relaxed and at ease. Mirroring speech patterns is a subtle way of indicating agreement and willingness to compromise. Consider utilising their name once or twice throughout the interview. When a person's name is mentioned in conversation, they typically respond with curiosity. It attracts their attention and fosters a feeling of closeness. Mentioning their name is effective, but avoid doing so excessively.

Imitation, also known as isopraxism, is mirrored. We imitate one another as a means of comforting one another, and you can observe this in humans (as well as some animals). By matching their speech patterns, body language, vocabulary, and tone—all unconscious processes—people can form bonds and establish trust. Rarely are you aware of the striking similarity between your posture when speaking with a new acquaintance and when conversing with an old friend at a party until someone points it out.

Fear of the unknown and attraction to the familiar are fundamental biological principles that explain our fascination with this phenomenon. Similar concepts apply to our attraction to similar individuals and concepts. This gives us a sense of security, as we know what to expect when we encounter someone who shares our values.

Positivity and realism

Being optimistic, genuine, and in touch with reality will set you apart in any circumstance. Do not speak negatively about your previous employer or anything else during the interview.

It may sound contradictory, but be honest about the aspects of your previous or current job that you did not enjoy. Speak neutrally about these issues and allow your interviewers to discern your core values. If you prefer to work independently and cannot tolerate being micromanaged, you should mention this in your interview. Your interviewers will appreciate your candour and will likely be motivated to share pertinent information about the position that will assist you in determining if it is a good fit.

Chapter 12: Creating An Outstanding Initial Impression When Meeting Your In-Laws

It can be intimidating to meet the family of your partner. The desire to impress your future in-laws can leave you feeling overwhelmed when you meet them for the first time. They will not form a complete opinion of you based solely on the initial impression, but how you present yourself during your initial meeting is crucial.

What your prospective in-laws think or feel about you after meeting you for the first time will have a significant impact on the nature of your long-term relationship with them.

To begin on the right foot, ensure that you:

Dress Appropriately

Although it may sound archaic, the way we dress is undoubtedly a form of communication. Putting forth a little extra effort in our appearance for special occasions demonstrates to others our respect for the occasion and the people involved. Wear something that allows you to unwind and have fun. Put on something that makes you feel confident and comfortable.

2. Bring a Present

Bring a present. Giving your in-laws a thoughtful present will help you make a favourable impression. It need not be something expensive. You are welcome to bring wine, cookies, or cake. Determine what your partner's family likes to avoid giving them an unappreciated gift.

3. Offer Compliments

Sincere compliments can win over individuals. Look around their home and compliment the furnishings, table setting, or artwork. Do not overdo it by complimenting everything you see; it can appear insincere if done excessively.

4. Speak distinctly

When meeting your in-laws for the first time, avoid being obnoxious and loud. Do not shout or use foul language. Pay close attention to your words and actions.

5. Behave yourself properly

Excessive use of good manners. There is no such thing as too much politeness, so long as it is genuine. Your in-laws are interested in how you treat their child, and small gestures such as saying "please" or offering to help with a small task can mean a great deal.

Concentrate on them

This family may soon become yours, so make an effort to become acquainted with them. Avoid being attached to your phone or partner. This is neither the time nor the place for public displays of affection (PDA), so avoid kissing and hugging your partner whenever possible. Focus for the time being on your family and independence.

Feel free to converse with various elderly and young family members. You can have fun with the children. Learn about your cousins, uncles, and aunts if they are present. This can be interpreted as an indication of your willingness to develop relationships with the extended family.

7. Demonstrate a Willingness to Assist

If you see an opportunity, ask where you can be of assistance. This is not about proving your worth or falling into a submissive dynamic immediately; rather, the objective is to demonstrate that you can participate as a member of the family.

8. Compliment Your Partner

The family will undoubtedly enjoy hearing about your partner's endearing characteristics. Praise your spouse before your in-laws.

9. Thank You

When it is time to depart, express gratitude for their hospitality. It is essential that they know you had a good time.

Be courteous to all members of the family.

If you are rude, they may ignore you or adopt an attitude that makes your visit unpleasant. Recognize your limitations and conduct yourself accordingly.

11. Avoid Sensitive Issues

Politics, money, sex, and religion are difficult to bring up in most conversations, and this one is no exception. If you are asked your opinion on a sensitive topic, feel free to share it. Recall the skill of active listening if tensions arise. Be genuine, be inquisitive, and respect the differences of others.

The purpose of the initial visit is to make a favourable impression. Instead of attempting to impress by sugarcoating your personality, be yourself and let them like you for who you are. Enjoy yourself, and eventually everything else will fall into place.

Chapter 13: Fundamentals Of Interaction

Conversational proficiency is essential in both your personal and professional lives. Whether you are communicating with people in public or at work, it is important to be mindful of how you do so. Here are some tips for having productive conversations:

When speaking in public, it is best to be courteous and respectful. When meeting someone for the first time, you should introduce yourself and, if possible, shake their hand. Maintain eye contact throughout the conversation and use positive body language, such as smiling and nodding when they speak. If the other person is friendly, don't be afraid to ask them questions that demonstrate genuine interest, such as "How did you become interested in this topic?" Keep in mind that conversations should flow naturally, so avoid interjecting or dominating the conversation with your own thoughts and opinions.

In the Workplace:

When communicating with coworkers, remember that professionalism is essential. If you have not already done so, introduce yourself and offer a handshake if appropriate. When asking for assistance or advice with something related to work projects, use formal language instead of slang and try not to take up too much of their time; practise clarity when explaining and patience when listening. Remain on track during meetings by bringing up pertinent topics and proposing solutions that could assist in achieving company goals; avoid discussing non-business topics unless invited to do so by other attendees. Always conclude conversations on a positive note, such as, "It was a pleasure speaking with you today!" We should keep in touch!

In Business:

Business conversations are interactions between two or more people that involve the exchange of business-related information or opinions. They may be formal or informal and cover topics including company policies, industry trends, project updates, and customer service. Good business conversations should be professional, courteous, and solution-oriented. They should also be receptive to different points of view and engage in active listening. Understanding the fundamentals of business conversation is essential for effective communication.

Conversations play a vital role in the development of effective communication skills, which are crucial for success in the business world. Understanding how to initiate and maintain a dialogue, listen to and respond to diverse perspectives, and frame conversations in a positive and productive manner can assist you in achieving your business objectives.

By understanding the fundamentals of business conversation, you can ensure productive interactions with colleagues, clients, and partners. This will help you build strong relationships, enhance your professional reputation, and establish a prosperous business.

Overall, being conscious of your communication skills and being respectful in conversations can help make conversations more productive. As with everything else, practise makes perfect, so don't be afraid to implement these tips!

How to Strategize Your Conversations

When interacting with others in public, at work, or in business, it is essential to maintain a respectful and professional demeanour. Here are some suggestions for ensuring that your conversations remain constructive:

It is essential to remember that being friendly is essential. Even if you do not know the person with whom you are speaking, be sure to acknowledge them politely. This can be as simple as saying "hello" or smiling when appropriate. Following these suggestions can help you communicate with others more amiably. Being cordial can facilitate the development of relationships, foster a positive environment, and make the conversation more enjoyable for both parties.

Ensure that you are actively listening to what the other person is saying and responding appropriately with questions and feedback. Listening demonstrates your interest in and respect for their viewpoints, while also providing you with additional insight into their perspectives on particular subjects.

Before diving into any question, make sure you understand what may be deemed appropriate or inappropriate for the given situation/environment. By doing so, you can ensure that your conversations remain respectful and do not cross any boundaries or make anyone feel uneasy.

4. Stay on topic: When conversing with someone at work or in public, unless the other person suggests otherwise, try to stick to one topic per conversation (s). This will enable all parties to maintain an organised conversation, rather than frequently veering off topic, which could

lead to misunderstandings or, worse, arguments!

5. Be concise and clear: Ensure that each point is presented succinctly and in a brief manner so that it is easily understood by whoever you are speaking with; rambling endlessly can cause confusion amongst listeners and frustration on their end as they may not have the time (or the patience) for such lengthy explanations!

A smile can go a long way in making someone feel accepted, respected, and welcome. It is a simple gesture that demonstrates your interest and willingness to engage in conversation. Smiling when approaching a conversation with someone is an excellent way to initiate a positive tone. It facilitates comfort and makes people feel welcome. Smiling also helps to create a welcoming environment and can make people more receptive to conversation. Additionally, it can assist in demonstrating that you are approachable and friendly, thereby increasing the likelihood that people will want to speak with you.

7. Maintain eye contact: Maintain eye contact when speaking with others. It indicates that you are attentive and interested in what they are saying.

This helps to demonstrate respect and create a more relaxed atmosphere. Eye contact also aids in establishing trust and rapport. However, it is important to be aware of the duration of your eye contact, as too much or too little can be perceived as uncomfortable or even aggressive. Maintaining eye contact is also a great way to demonstrate engagement and attentiveness in a conversation.

Maintaining eye contact when approaching a conversation is crucial to establishing an effective and positive exchange.

Utilize words that are uplifting and encouraging in conversation. Avoid using language that may be interpreted as negative or critical. It is important to use positive language when approaching a conversation to ensure a productive and respectful exchange. Positive language can help create a sense of mutual understanding and trust, as well as set the tone for a productive conversation. Positive conversations can be facilitated through the use of uplifting language, attentive listening, and an openness to different points of view. In addition, avoiding negative language such as criticism, sarcasm, and judgement can contribute to the success of a conversation. Lastly, it is essential to be conscious of the language you employ and any potential misunderstandings or misinterpretations that could arise. By using positive language, you can help create a safe, respectful, and productive atmosphere for the exchange of ideas between both parties.

Use open body language. Open body language, such as uncrossed arms and a relaxed posture, communicates that you are at ease and open to conversation. It is essential to approach a conversation with open body language. Open body language indicates to the other person that you are interested and engaged in the conversation.

These are examples of expressive body language:

•Smiling and maintaining a relaxed facial expression •Keeping arms uncrossed •Leaning towards the other person •Facing the other person directly •Using

hand gestures to emphasise points
- Asking open-ended questions

Using open body language will create a more comfortable and relaxed environment, allowing for a more effective conversation.

Conversation will flow naturally, and the other person will be more likely to participate. By utilising expressive body language, you can foster an environment of mutual respect and trust. This will facilitate a more fruitful discussion.

It is essential to use open body language when initiating conversations in order to make the other person feel comfortable and valued. This will contribute to the creation of a positive environment, which will ultimately result in a more productive conversation.

When approaching a conversation with another person, it is essential to be genuine. Start by taking the time to get to know the person and establishing a safe, comfortable environment. Ask them about their interests and life, and pay close attention to their responses. Demonstrate interest in what they have to say and respect for their viewpoints, even if they differ from yours. In your communication, be sincere and genuine, and avoid making assumptions. Finally, be willing to share your own experiences and emotions, even if they differ from those of the other person. Be yourself; do not pretend to be someone else. In relationship-building, sincerity is of great value.

These actions will help you establish a climate of trust and can lead to profound conversations.

By adhering to these guidelines and remaining mindful of your conversations, you can ensure that any professional or public interaction remains respectful and fruitful.

B. Establishing Relations with Others

Establishing rapport with others in public and at work is essential to fostering positive relationships and achieving success professionally. Rapport is the sense of connection, trust, comprehension, and respect that exists between two or more individuals. Establishing a positive rapport with others facilitates improved communication, increased cooperation and collaboration, and enhanced problem-solving abilities.

There are several steps you can take to establish successful connections and relationships when establishing rapport with others in public or at work. First, be courteous! A greeting with a smile or a kind word sets a positive tone that can go a long way toward establishing a healthy rapport. When communicating with others, whether a coworker or a friend, active listening is essential to achieving genuine shared comprehension. This entails giving each person your undivided attention by looking them in the eye, nodding as they speak (to demonstrate comprehension), and asking thoughtful questions to demonstrate your interest in the discussion.

Focusing on common ground rather than differences is another important aspect of building relationships based on rapport; while we all have unique opinions and life experiences that shape who we are as individuals, finding topics where everyone has similar views can help bridge potential divides before they become an issue. Even when discussing contentious topics, demonstrate mutual respect by validating each other's viewpoints rather than becoming defensive or attacking beliefs (even if only through body language).

One of the most helpful tips for establishing a positive rapport is to demonstrate genuine appreciation for the efforts of those around you, from major accomplishments such as completing projects to small acknowledgments such as complimenting someone's outfit as you pass them on the street. Even though these may appear to be inconsequential actions on their own, they add up over time to create a larger impression of a person's genuine interest in building relationships as opposed to merely complying with workplace/public setting norms.

Building a positive rapport begins slowly but will continue to pay dividends for years to come, so put forth your best effort every day.

Active listening and asking open questions

Active listening is an important skill in both public and professional settings because it enables individuals to demonstrate that they are genuinely interested in understanding the speaker's perspective, rather than simply trying to persuade them. Active listening entails more than simply hearing the other person's words. It involves nonverbal attention, asking pertinent follow-up questions, restating what the speaker said, and demonstrating comprehension. Open questions, those that require more than a yes or no response and encourage dialogue between the two parties, can be particularly useful in this situation.

In a public setting, open questions can facilitate conversations with strangers and help people get to know one another better by encouraging a more in-depth examination of topics. Questions such as "What made you decide...?" or "Can you tell me more about...?" allow people to make connections beyond surface-level topics and can lead to a deeper understanding of a person's ideas and beliefs.

In the workplace, asking open-ended questions and engaging in active listening are essential for productive conversations about challenging topics such as performance feedback or when collaborating on projects involving team disagreements. In such situations, employees require assurance that their opinions are being heard in order for significant changes or solutions to be implemented. Actively listening without interruption through body language cues such as eye contact and nods as well as restating what was said prior to asking open-ended follow-up questions enables all participants in the conversation to feel heard while gathering the necessary information from all parties in order to generate creative solutions that are acceptable to all parties.

Active listening and open-ended questions create an environment conducive to meaningful conversation, whether in a public or professional setting. These skills can be used to better connect people and build relationships, as well as uncover more information, which can lead to productive collaboration and solutions.

D. Maintaining the Conversation

Maintaining a conversation in public and at work is an important skill that can facilitate the development of strong relationships with coworkers, colleagues, and other individuals. When out in public, such as at a restaurant with friends or on a date, it is essential to be able to keep the conversation going. You must also possess this skill in the workplace. Maintaining lively and engaging conversations with coworkers can strengthen relationships and make working together more enjoyable for everyone.

It is essential to initiate conversations by being genuine and candid about your interests. Don't just talk about yourself; ask the other person questions as well! Posing thoughtful questions can lead to a deeper understanding of each other's perspectives, which can facilitate the formation of long-lasting relationships.

It is important to pay attention when people are speaking in both social and professional settings so that you can respond appropriately. When someone shares something important to them or tells a story, demonstrate respect by offering your own input or experiences and asking pertinent follow-up questions. This will keep the conversation lively and interesting for both parties.

When conversing with others, it is also advantageous to demonstrate sensitivity towards differing opinions, even if they differ from your own, without engaging in debates over divisive topics such as politics or religion, which could potentially cause discord in a setting where everyone must remain focused on a shared objective: completing tasks efficiently and effectively together.

By practising active listening skills and expressing genuine interest in others' points of view while maintaining healthy boundaries regarding personal beliefs and values, you will go a long way toward keeping conversations alive and fostering meaningful relationships, whether in public with friends or at work with coworkers!

Chapter 14: Self-Assurance Does Not Come Naturally

I recall a leader I admired in my mid-20s telling me that my shyness may hinder my ability to lead others. My initial reaction was negative. Because shyness had always been portrayed as a social weakness, I felt defensive. However, upon reflection, I realised that he had hit the nail on the head.

My timidity was deeply rooted in history. My mother's suicide, which occurred when I was still a young boy, utterly destroyed my self-assurance. Life began to feel too unpredictable to seize with both hands and maximise. It was unquestionably safer for me to stay within my small bubble and only explore the familiar. Unfortunately, my goals were so lofty that I had to overcome my shyness and fear of the unknown in order to achieve them.

You may have had a different childhood than I did, but you may have experienced a few life events that shook your confidence or reinforced your fears, making it seem too risky to venture outside your comfort zone. Thankfully, despite all that you have endured, you had the courage to pursue your dream of becoming an entrepreneur. However, now is the time to become an even more confident leader!

You may be surprised to learn that confidence is not something that people are born with. It is developed through your attitudes and experiences in life. Self-confidence is a tool that facilitates communication and enables leaders to exert influence over others, so leaders teach themselves how to develop it. Before I started my own business, I began working with a variety of mentors and leaders who taught me how to lead meetings and speak in front of various groups. This allowed me to practise confidence, as opposed to simply reading about it or understanding it intellectually.

In addition, I was able to assess my presentations and identify areas for improvement. Due to my lack of self-confidence, eye contact was not one of my strong points. It was difficult for me to look people in the eyes without becoming distracted or incredibly self-conscious! I quickly realised that my inability to maintain eye contact gave others the impression that I wasn't interested in them. Instead of completely avoiding eye contact, I would look just above or at people's noses.

When I describe the lengths I have gone to cultivate confidence, it may sound absurd, but the point is to demonstrate that developing confidence requires effort on your part. Similar to listening, it is a skill that must be developed over time. Depending on your past experiences and personality, practising confidence may force you to venture far outside of your comfort zone. However, one of the most effective ways to develop confidence is to intentionally place oneself in uncomfortable situations.

Do what frightens you. I assure you that you will not regret it. Even if the desired outcomes are not attained, you can still look back and see evidence of your courage. Friend, this is how you can increase your self-confidence!

Not Always Will It Feel Good

We frequently assume that being talented or successful automatically confers confidence, but you would be surprised by the number of talented athletes, musicians, and businesspeople who have accomplished extraordinary feats but still struggle with low self-esteem.

David Bowie, the legendary English musician and songwriter, once disclosed that when he finally attained superstar status and began packing concert halls with fervent fans, he struggled with self-image issues. Only when he was performing on stage or obsessively writing at home did he feel good. This was due to the fact that his self-assurance was tied to what he did (composing, recording, and performing music) rather than who he was as a multifaceted person.

These examples make me hesitant to advise others to "fake it until you make it." Certainly, feigning confidence can be a short-term lifesaver, and you can fool a great number of people. The only person you cannot deceive is yourself. How will you feel when you leave the office and all the confidence you've displayed for the past nine hours evaporates? Or, what will occur when an unanticipated business opportunity forces you outside your comfort zone?

True confidence will not always feel good because it requires you to be honest and open about who you are; therefore, stop pretending! Nobody expects you to give your heart to others or lose your identity, but you must be crazy enough to believe in your abilities, see the world and others in a positive light, and pursue your goals with conviction. Training yourself to become truly confident requires effort, but here are three strategies you can begin implementing daily:

Acknowledge both your strengths and weaknesses. It is typical to embrace the aspects of oneself that are praised by others and conceal those that embarrass one. However, presenting an image of perfection only induces insecurity and the fear of being exposed one day. It is preferable to be your genuine self (flaws and all) and allow others to get to know the real you.

Put yourself in uncomfortable circumstances. The more you confront your fears, the less fearful you will become. The belief that your fears are more powerful than you is what keeps them alive, and a portion of you believes you would perish if they materialised. Expose yourself on purpose to situations that make you feel uncomfortable, and observe how capable and competent you are in these circumstances.

- Practice becoming more receptive. There is an art to establishing rapport. You should share just enough information to keep a conversation going and allow others to get to know you better, but not so much that you reveal deeply personal or sensitive details. One of the most effective ways to break the ice is to create opportunities to discuss topics that interest you. Attend specialised conferences, participate in specialised forum discussions, or join a professional interest group or club. You will gain the confidence to share your thoughts and experiences, as well as hone your listening abilities!

Chapter 15: Avoid Making Assumptions

Presumptions can destroy relationships, and in fact, they do exactly that. Suspicions can be instantaneous or irrational. An immediate supposition that is fundamentally an individual's belief, regardless of the veracity of the belief. The concept may have no actual relationship, but the individual believes the concept to be true and consequently answers based on their beliefs.

Then, there are the convoluted assumptions. These are assumptions derived from an external source, which we accept as accurate recycled information. Recycled information is rarely reliable, yet people frequently assume that what they hear from others is accurate. The reason recycled information is rarely accurate is due to the fact that in discussions, people tend to hear only the parts that are relevant to their emotions at the time, and when they transfer it to others, it is unrelated to the topic at hand and merely reflects the information as they heard it, not as fate intended.

A belief in which there is no proof. Here are some examples of assumptions that can harm relationships.

a) Accepting that you are being disadvantaged

b) Accepting people are persistently attempting to obtain money from you

c) Accepting that you are being ignored

d) Accepting that your soul mate comprehends your thoughts

There are others, but these are the most common misconceptions that harm relationships. The inherent problem with any kind of presumption that feeling satisfaction is all there is to it, which inevitably elicits a local response. When we anticipate a piece of information, we respond in light of it. Negative presumptions do not, however, simply appear out of nowhere; they are typically prompted by our own feelings of fear. For instance, a person who believes that others are attempting to extort money from them likely has a general aversion to other people using them (trust issues) and a profound aversion to money. This causes them to search for indications of being used for money (whether or not this is actually the case) and to respond to individuals based on these presumptions.

For example, Jerry, a man in his fifties with a demanding job that occasionally keeps him out until 11 p.m. Since he was frequently out so late, his wife, Jill, suspected he was cheating on her as their relationship struggled. She suspected he was unfaithful for two reasons: an immediate presumption and an indirect suspicion.

Jill had been concerned for some time, based on her own life experience, that men are deviants and that Jerry would sooner or later cheat on her and leave her. So, when she began to receive signals that triggered her separation anxiety, the predetermined assumption was that she was being abandoned. This was her psychological condition being fulfilled by a false notion. It's critical to know that since individuals feel an inclination doesn't be guaranteed to mean it's exact to the circumstance (this is normally found in fears where individuals feel dread, however are really protected. This likewise works the other way around, an individual can have a solid sense of reassurance while as yet being in harm's way). Since Jill felt deserted doesn't mean she was being deserted.

The roundabout suspicion in this situation was Jill's companion, who saw Jerry at a café with a lady while he should be at a conference. Jill's companion quickly called Jill and revealed this to her. What the companion didn't know was that the lady Jerry was out to supper with was the conference. However, with Jill's psychological condition being the need to satisfy a dream of being deserted, she previously expected that her companion's data was precise — that this was a date beyond the marriage, instead of a conference — no matter what the truth.

What prompts poisonousness is when individuals take these suspicions and run with them. At the point when individuals have a profound psychological condition (like Jill's "need" to be deserted), individuals become so connected to these requirements that they really favor their suppositions rather than the real world, when in this close to home space. They'd prefer trust the prattle, or maybe accept their own considerations over the real factors since it approves the feelings that they, as a matter of fact "need" to encounter.

I view this as very normal with individuals in conditions of outrage. When irate, individuals will quite often search for data that will approve and propagate their displeasure, as opposed to determine the issue (maybe on the grounds that it would be too disgracing and humiliating to gain proficiency with their resentment depends on something not situated actually) (maybe on the grounds that it would be too disgracing and humiliating to gain proficiency with their resentment depends on something not situated actually).

The more suspicions individuals make and accept, the better opportunity this will hinder all connections — heartfelt, yet with family, companions, and even ourselves, too. Individuals' presumptions can flow into a snowball of unrealities, and soon, it becomes hazy what we've appeared in our own selves and what has really occurred truly.

www.ingramcontent.com/pod-product-compliance
Lightning Source LLC
Chambersburg PA
CBHW050253120526
44590CB00016B/2329